In His Words

by C. Emmanuel Griffin

Five Sisters Publishing

www.fivesisterspublishing.com
First Edition: January 2023
Published in North America by Five Sisters Publishing. For information, please contact Five Sisters Publishing, c/o Anita Royston, P.O. Box 217, Gretna, Virginia, 24557.

Library of Congress Cataloguing-In-Publication Data   2013952224

In His Words/C. Emmanuel Griffin – 1st ed

ISBN: 978-1-941859-87-2

1. RELIGION / Christian Living / Inspirational. 2. RELIGION / Christian Living / Personal Growth. 3. BODY, MIND & SPIRIT / Inspiration & Personal Growth. 4. PHILOSOPHY / Free Will & Determinism. 5. POETRY / American / African American & Black.

10   9   8   7   6   5   4   3   2   1

Comments about *In His Words* and requests for additional copies, book club rates and author speaking appearances may be addressed to C. Emmanuel Griffin or Five Sisters Publishing c/o Anita Royston, P.O. Box 217, Gretna, Virginia, 24557, or you can send your comments and requests via e-mail to clarence.e.griffin@twintermite.com

Also available as an eBook from Internet retailers and from Five Sisters Publishing

Printed in the United States of America

Appreciation

I want to thank my mother, Anita L. Royston, who always believed and encouraged me to write and tell stories about my adventures in life. She is my first teacher in the imaginative arts.

A special thanks to all the family and friends, who have supported me along the way. Their support means more than they will ever know. Lastly, a special thanks to my incredible friend, Graham Goddard, who interpreted each poem in a way only he could.

Table of Contents

To The Reader

This book is the culmination of over 10 years of thoughtful consideration of the ideas, experiences, and circumstances that I have been blessed to encounter thus far in life.

I truly believe that each and every one of us has, or will have, an incredible story to tell. And I pray that one day that I will have the opportunity to share in your experiences, as you are sharing in mine.

And Action...

Upon this stage
The joy, love, passion and rage
Crafted and tweaked
Every syllable of speech
Refined for the moment in time
Appropriate for every occasion
Orchestrated by the One behind the lens
Celebrations of loved ones and friends
Barbecues and family reunions
Weddings, graduations and funerals too
The scenes may blend as we pretend
The actors may come and go off screen
Live is this feature without repeating
Forever is space without the gap of deleting
Accountable to the Most High, who rates
Every move every thought every intention
Silent he will listen and advise in spirit tongue
And demonstrate the strength of the faithful
Of the meek
Granted are we who assume the chair
The star of the dramatization not observed there
Ever-present as the Comforters hand
Pruning for purpose each second as time
Nothing is wasted, waste is not-a-thing
But a resource and a recourse to be utilized
As a mistake is but a break from the euthanized state
Where time and space cooperate
Where opportunities and emergencies just wait
There just there off screen
In the creative creator's mind unseen
Sits the director with this whole universe in view
Holding but a brilliant realization
The team, the actors, the camera crew
The joy the pain demonstrated like new
All and all they say, think, do
Pontificate as sound and wind
Upon the meaning and desires of you.

And Action

The Fire This Time

The Fire this Time

John said, I baptize with water
But the one who comes after me
Will baptize with the fire of the Holy Spirit
That fire will enter your bones and won't let you alone
It will infiltrate your dreams and begin to build a fortress
of strategic ideas for the coming day
It will help you run and not be weary
It will feed you from the nutrient richness of its essence
It will guide you like a pillar of fire through the night or
A God-filled cloud during the day
Yes, the fire this time is one that
Will blind ignorance to its opportunity
The fire this time will not be extinguished with a single shot
The fire this time is one that cannot die
Because it was lit by the Almighty
And this fire cannot lie because in it is
A light that exposes the truth in every seen and unseen stronghold
And every blood diamond and stolen artifact-filled vault
The fire this time as the prophet James Baldwin expressed
Was even beyond his understanding
Like the temple that was torn down and restored in three days
This fire will set this whole world ablaze
But it will not destroy what God has built
It will purify and relieve all guilt
Along with the burden of ill-gotten gains
Stored up for the poor for the season of rains
To care for the poor, widows and orphaned
And necessitating the fulfillment of
The contract of 40 acres and a mule
This is the fire that burns on a fuel
Of justice, civil justice and just law as a rule.

The Mission

The Mission

What if God sent you on a secret mission into the world to secure
And improve the life's conditions of a specific population of his children
How would you move, how would you occupy your time, how would you
prepare for your battles and challenges
Would you read the Bible, Dante and Voltaire
Would you read the adventurous works of Dumas
Would you curate your dietary intake to make sure that
You take in calories that yield the greatest value energetically
Would you daily get plenty of water and adequate hours of sleep
How would you manage your relationships?
Would you always seek to be, in every conversation right
Or would you be prudent and always
Keep the mission's objective firmly in sight
Would you stress with anxiety over engagements gone amiss
Or would you have the presence of mind to remain vigilant and focused
What is your mission? What is your plan
You are more than a soul, you are greater than a man
See your time as a clock that is ticking
And bind your actions to a rod of values worth sticking
And learn and learn and acquire and acquire with skill and ability
And intellectual dexterity and eyes that see clearly this moments reality
You have work to do God's children are dependent on you
Be disciplined and move like the wind, felt and yet unseen
Move in the crowd but keep your substantial constitutional properties
And never fear and never veer from the path of the plan
God has given you   your orders and in this you cannot fail
As long as to your creator's heart, mind and spirit you constantly avail.

C. Emmanuel Griffin

INNER PEACE

If it is inner peace that you seek
Start by welcoming the Prince of Peace into your heart
Then with every heartbeat, with every breath you breathe
There will be an expression of the Most High, the Son of Man
And everyone you meet will feel the power within
Because it is the renewable power that never lies and never dies
Everyone is searching for the truth and if you
Invite Him into your heart and into your mind
They will find it in you, because out of the heart the mouth speaks
And your words will give clues that lead others to their truth
And you will find yourself surrounded by friends and sisters and brothers
Because the truth leads all to one place
And you will never be alone because the truth has but one home
And at the feet of the Father all who have accepted the
Risen king, the redeemer who lives, and the way the truth and the life
Will be enjoined into the great collective
So invite Jesus Christ into your life and have
The inner peace you so desire
With him inside your heart you will always be in the majority
And on the side of right as you say, and you do in obedience
And with the authority you have been given
So invite Jesus into your heart and have the inner peace you deserve
And watch how everything around you changes
And begins to bend toward you as others feel the presence
That you by choice and force of your will have made resident
In the sacred space in your heart, and everywhere you go, every place
You are found will be instantly, made Holy Ground
You are empowered to be the light that shines so bright
That to others are reviled that the choice and opportunity
For the peace and freedom they seek
Is within reach of the sound of their voice
Or the safety of their thoughts
And all they have to do, like you
Is welcome the Prince of Peace into their hearts.

Inner Peace

In Defense of You

In Defense of You

The mother's creed
From birth
To my child
My earth
Everything I do is in defense of you
There is no element permitted
Into the space of your life acquitted
That poses a threat to your well being
Whether in good nature, intention or in well meaning

I will erect a wall
You protect you even against yourself
In me God planted an oracle
With knowledge of origins even I don't know
But just as true as the light of blue
Everything I do is in defense of you
No one again will pass this place
Presenting poison apples to steal promise from your race
And even when I am long gone from earthly sight
My words and actions will rotate in your mind
And in those moments the peace you seek you will find
And the words you need to summon as subject to the royal chamber
Will come to you willingly and present their gifts
To protect you from the ground that constantly shifts
Building bridges of paragraphs over cavernous terrain
Shielding you from the injustice of glutinous self-serving pain
Everything I do is in defense of you
This seed I give and pray that in fertile soil you sew it
And one day we will see
As we look back from seat of eternity
That the essence of my time was true
And all that I said, did, hoped, cried, bled for
Was all done
In defense of you.

C. Emmanuel Griffin

Force of Faith

There are Four Natural Forces we are told
But this, my friend, is an unfortunate lie
There is another buried within our code
Which keeps us traveling upon life's road
If you apply it, it will serve you well
If you deny it, it will surely tell
Everywhere and to everyone exposed
In the friends and associates you chose
Day as light evidently clear
Susceptible to the threats of lack and fear
Open to the ways of slight-of-hand
Subject to the trickery of the thieving plan
But of course there is a simple and accessible remedy
All you have to do is believe
And then
The Force of Faith will be your friend
Your Ally in your quest to be
The embodiment of your ancestors' dreams
In full and utter self-control
Body and Mind Heart and Soul
In ounce of it is all you need
Mountains moved by mustard seed
This will move the entire planet to rest
Jesus Christ was ego less
He said with Faith we would outdo his best
And in this Word
I challenge you to test
In your coming and going you will be blessed
And your prayers will be efficient and will impact much
Golden will be your words and platinum will be your touch.

Force of Faith

Mine

Would you abandon a diamond mine
Just because in your lifetime
Not a single shining object did you find
What if God had said
Long after you are dead
Your faithful and diligent descendants
Would one day uncover what has been there all along
Would you keep working
Knowing that the only gift of wealth
You will pass on is knowledge of mining
And the example of faith and health
Would you keep digging for the goal
Knowing that your spirit will reap
What your body and soul have sown
If you knew it would take 500 years
To receive your recognition and reward
To be validated in the eyes of those
Who depend on the fluid of air to breathe
Would you keep working through the pain and the hurt
Knowing that you will only be unearthing dirt
That you would be laughed at and, mocked and ridiculed
Would you keep working the mine
Would you invest all of your time

In His Words

If you knew that you
Or those coming through your line
Would one day find
A single jewel that would reflect
The light of the universe's first glimmer
That would shine so bright that it would be
As if holding a star in the palm of your hand
And looking at the essence of eternity
Would you keep digging
Would you hold on to the promise
Would you be faithful to the spirit that cannot lie
If you do and are able to
You will hear in your quite contemplative moments
A faint vibration of absolute truth

C. Emmanuel Griffin

What is yours is mine
What is mine is yours
You are here and there
You are there and here
See through my eyes
And you will see through the disguise
You have all the time
Beyond what is known or shown
Hold the line
And you will find
What you seek
Is already known
Keep digging.

Mine

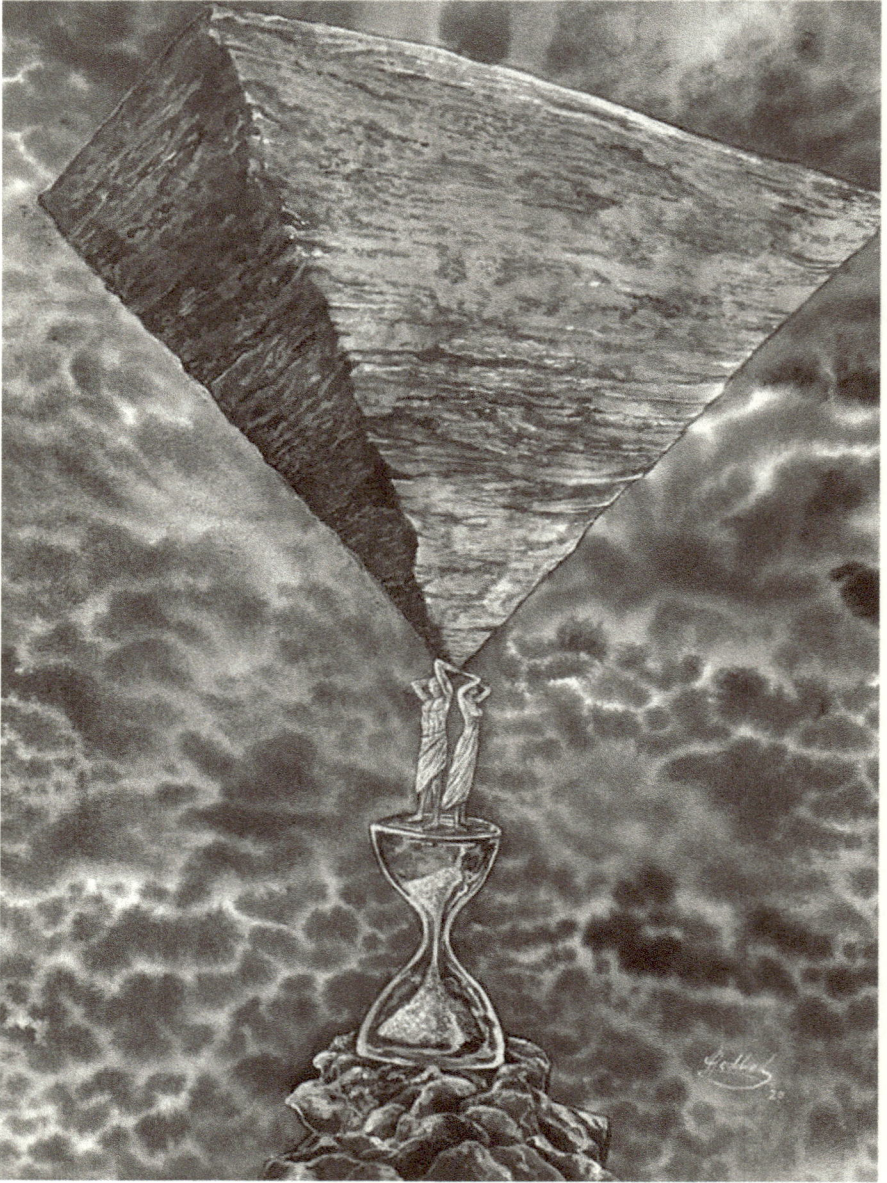

Upon A Point

Upon a Point

I saw a vision of the Great Pyramid upside down
balancing upon a single point
And if we, citizens of humanity, ever want to be free, then
We must release our minds of doubt,
that if we trust we will be left without
We must recognize that the established facts
given to us with restrictive intention are built on a foundation of lies
We are told that it's gravity that holds this whole world together
but again a fiction, like that of the man, who with his hands
builds a prison of codified laws, with invisible lines demarcating walls
with punishments and perilous predicaments
facing thousands who dare to traverse
But the simple solution to this generational curse
Is this, put your hand in my hand and leave it there
Never let space grown between us
Make the will of time and it's forcefulways flow
like fluid air around us
And let us take another's hand,
and let us make a global band
of those that look just like us, who fear more than death
The loss of the sacred trust, that comes from letting go
On a single point we can hold, the ever-expanding pyramid
of knowledge to build a work that like the first
Still the mind confounds, which will stand the test of time
and others will come and stand online
and seek our council again this time,
differently, without the possibility, of disfiguring
our edifices or misnomering our names or going back
to where they come from and claiming
our truths and discoveries as eminences from their brains
This time, because of the work of our minds, all will know
though may not understand, that they have learned
a life sustained truth from the bonded band of those
that got from this very spot the chance to see the beautiful, warm
golden, morning birth of impossibilities improvisation.

C. Emmanuel Griffin

12:00:00

This is the first second, of the first day
Of the rest of your conscious life
This is the moment in time and space that you realize that
You are a creator and there is a Creator
All that you desire can be made or acquired for a price
You must ask yourself before you
Engage in any exchange of your
Precious time, for a goal or wage
how much am I willing to pay
Everything has an energy cost
There is always a gain or a loss
and everything is always completely full
and the question is, *with what*
Open your mind Your mind is a virtual machine
You can contain a limitless innumerable constellation of things
thoughts, talents, skills, abilities, insights, and senses
You are a creator, so consciously create
Count the cost and begin the work
The world was made in 7 days
Don't be afraid to believe
Fear is but a system that believes in doubt
Faith is but a system that believes in limitless possibilities
Create! Go and do greater things
This is your endless destiny
See where it goes and enjoy the views
from valleys and plateaus now unknown
Today is the first second of the first day
Imagine and realize the possibilities
in this time and space and all that is to come
from within the infinite chasm of you.

12:00:00

Philosophy

Philosophy

Truth is verifiable
Like length and distance
When we agree let it be the measure
Take a thing, a simple string
Call it a unit we treasure as true
And in equal parts divide up what we are due
Let our words exact from our hearts
That which our hearts demand from our souls
Which to each was given a spirit of which
The connection to all things holds
Let there be simplicity in all our expressions of love
Speak together we of acknowledged dreams gifted and formed
Aligned from the ground to the clouds
Making communication a fabrication
Of the relation of light and sound.

C. Emmanuel Griffin

Let our words to all be as exciting as lightning
Because it draws its essence and authority from that power
Is in one be in all and in all be as one
Let your time be the teller of the tales
Which before conception are effectively already done
For the reason the only treason is the abstraction in fear of fact
We will get there when we unburden and unpack
That the teachers are the students and learning is turning back
To the place where and the pace that limitations were but imitations
Of the elements of bridges lacked
And imagination was the station where life's journey chose its clothes
And our suppositions and conditions were but selections of collective prose
And with this we must bear witness to the distress of the time
Which is calling our attention to
The perpetrator of the tragedy of THE crime
When force colluded and silenced the olfactory sense of fact
Beyond reason is the refusal to acknowledge the contributions of those
Who laid the foundation of the nations that today many call home

In His Words

But where there is an illness
In the stillness there rests a cure
Do not waver from the truth
Do not favor the rich and powerful
And let the story be told in appreciation
And let humanity in solidarity with
A never-before observed clarity
Our advantage and disadvantage
In our thoughts and actions
Birthed of unequal measures
Outside of the line
Incapable of legitimate proof
In this
And only this
Are all
Or will we ever be Free.

Distraction

Yes Dis-trac-tion is the tool that moves our minds away
from our goals or objectives
It is this getting off-track that holds us back

Eliminate the distractions in education or any situation
And you will arrive at a station of thought, creation or realization
Which will propel you beyond the challenges you face

So much time we waste getting back on-track
So I say let's eliminate all things in our lives
That move us away from seeing clearly
And focusing on our goals

If the distraction is money or the lack thereof
Or people, or phones, or relationships more complex
We need to move them off of our track
So that we are not dis-tracked
And therefore miss our stated destination

Distraction is the only tool of the Evil One
That spirit knows it cannot touch your soul
It can only, like a phantom, place false facts
And imaginary objects in your path

See through the tricks and keep traveling down
Your blessed tracks toward the greatness
That was placed upon your life
Even before you possessed it.

Distraction

C. Emmanuel Griffin

Noah's Arc

This is not a tale about destruction
It is a blueprint for success
First of all, listen to God alone and ignore
The distractions from all the rest
Start with a small group, two or three will suffice
God will provide what you need as well as the best advice
Make your location upon a hill and discard every ill device
Then prepare and build and care for the assignment
As if life depended upon it
As if all of humanity depended on it
Build something that everyone can understand and recognize
That this is an ONLY GOD production
God is waiting for you to do your part
He has the riches of the world and the universe
Waiting on you to do your part
The Flood is coming, the fire is coming too
The flood of blessings is coming and like
The blood it's passing through
If you are wise, it will not drown but carry you
High above all that you ever knew
And when God sends his sign you will know
That the time has come to build again
Look around and survey the land
Don't worry about who on it now stands
See with the eyes of God the timeline of the affairs of man
From this cerebral height design the plan
From this depth of feeling lay your foundation
Beyond wealth and beyond persuasion
In this space see the unseen which lay just beyond
The spectrum of common understanding
In this life all in pairs and bunches you can get it
The only difference is your unyielding commitment.

Noah's Arc

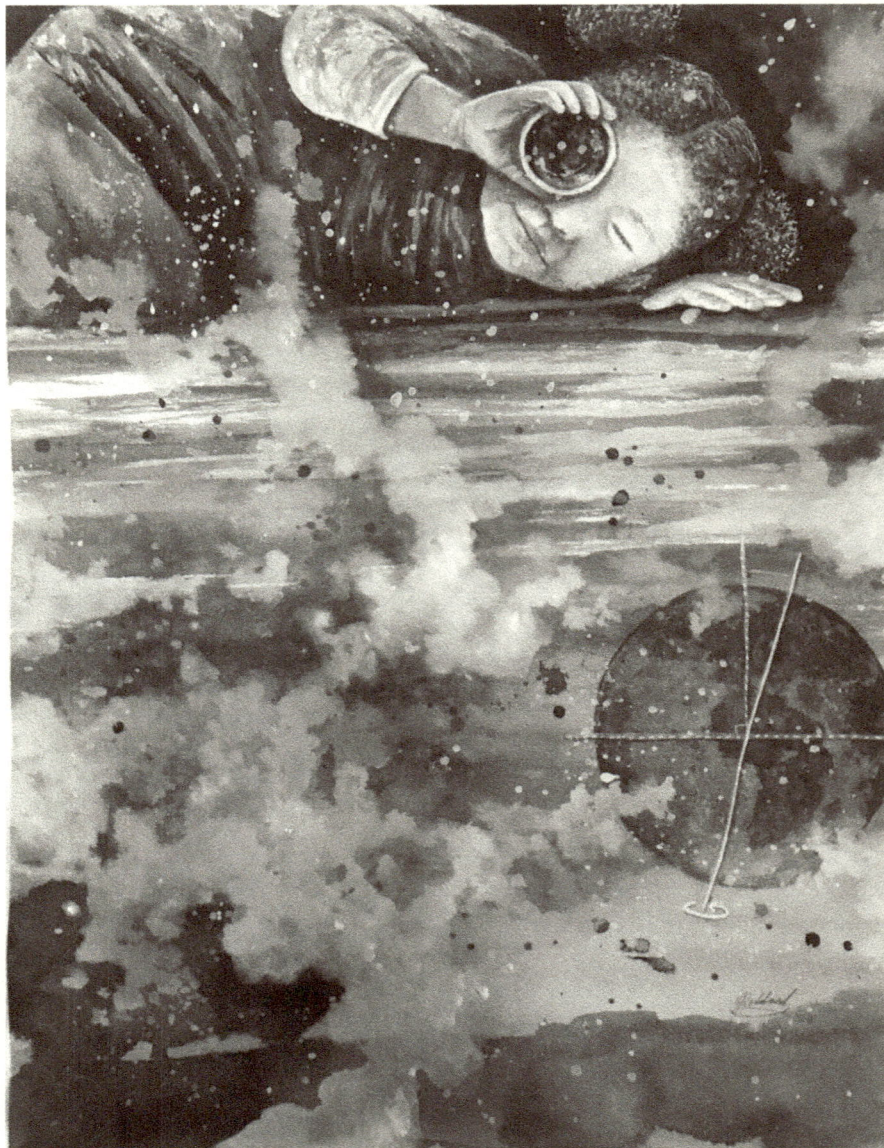

Look 23

Look 23

Recognize that life like the world is tilted
It leans and revolves around the most massive
It rotates   around a single point
And repeats itself by degrees of 15
Making one day of 24 hours just like the next
We must recognize that time is not lost or wasted
Time like age is but a figment of our collective imagination
All things grow and wither and change form
Nothing is created or destroyed just recycled and repurposed
Don't worry about what you will be
After this probably fodder for a tree
That's why I say take my ashes and bury me
And on top of my grave plant a cherry tree
That way this body will be
Useful even after the transformation
But let's look at what we do before that point

C. Emmanuel Griffin

The wisdom of this world is absolutely foolish
The ones who recognize this soonest will be the happiest
Sadness and madness come from a separation of truth from reality
The energy cost is not reflected or related to one's salary
Working hard is not a noble art
That's a lie and not even smart
Working for your passion is the central heart
That's where the life force resides in the ventral part

The rich are just a reflection of the more massive or the more dense
It's the game we know and hate to play
But we feel the benefit of imbalance and we use it
To our advantage when we have it
The issue is having a plan to utilize the mass
Gained through collective purpose and action
Or else comes the fated lesson taught by the atom
Too much of one thing makes unstable
And radioactive and decay
Is but a song sung before the ringing of the bell
Which opens the gates to the pit where hopes fell

In His Words

Look not at me Look 23 degrees
That's the plane and the level
Tilt the page and begin to write
This life a new story for a new age
This is the gap in human history that all epochs must have
This is the new beginning
This is the silent period where souls have chance to reconnect
With the living and God spoke louder than ever before

Follow the pattern not of man but of the
Earth's plan by design
And incline or recline
Depending on where you find
Yourself and see the path we are taking
No more separation or breaking, each of us is
Banking on the same shores and each of us
Has our own ore in the river of this time

Get in on this ship this time
Partner with the team this time
And let a lacking of love be the only crime
Punishable by death, guilty of excluding faith
As the guiding light by which we make!

Just Position

Just Position

What if you had a book of rules and instructions
That would empower you with the skills to actively
And consciously control, the body, mind, spirit and soul
Well, here it is: The Kingdom of Heaven is within You
Your body is the organic limitation, mode of transportation
In which you physically and temporarily exist
In relation to the outside world
Your mind is the semi-physical representation of your soul
Which is dispersed throughout your being from your skin to your core
Your soul is the consciousness, the awareness
That goes beyond the observable via mechanical operations
Of physical organs and organ systems
The spirit is the seat of ultimate control and connection
To the Creator of all that is, was, and will be
What if someone offered you the key
And it was completely free
Would you take it

So here is assumption
As in to assume
Not as in observation that lacks sufficient thought, or concrete facts
But as in position Assume the position and your entire being
Will flow in that direction as if on the top of a slope

C. Emmanuel Griffin

Try this lie down on your right-hand side and observe how you feel
That is the Soul's side, where it taps into the deep emotions
That keep residence at the border of awake and rejuvenating sleep
And there exists the generation of creative rich concepts and ideas
Try it and feel the flow of your breath come and go,
Out and in like a river or an ocean as it waxes and wanes

Lie on your back and pull your limbs close to the center
This alignment is the focal point of the spirit
That is a signal sender and receiver like light
And is not bound by gravity
This is a position of connectivity
Your soul is aligned when your focus is upward,
That is away from the gravity of the ground (or worries)
That hold your physical body down tight
In this position you can organize the stars of the galaxy
Or more practically, your thoughts, which are just as immense,
And make plans of action that are clear because
The spirit is that part of God that has no fear of life
Which is all that is

In His Words

Pay attention, use all your powers of observation
Watch yourself as you move throughout the day
Are your hands balled into fist
What are you holding onto that needs to be released
Are your arms crossed
What are you defending or protecting
The last example I will share is the position of prayer
Some kneel some, some stand
Some form circles and hold hands
Some clasp their fingers and palms
And others look to the sky
This is a powerful position that connects and orchestrates,
Because the one who everything makes and makes everything
Is listening, and from within and beyond will respond vibrationally
With an energy and frequency that unmistakably moves mountains

With Every movement, be vigilant
Don't attempt to use this as a tool
To control or convict others
That's useless
Use this to discover
All the missing pieces of you
That are lost in every second of time
Unknowingly reacting to the outside world
I could go on and on with examples of what
Every movement and motion mean and indicate
In terms of thought, intent, emotion or feeling
But that would defeat the purpose of the journey of
Discovering and recovering your God-given plot
In the story of the Heaven that is within you
Just position yourself in all things
In thought, in word, in action, for success
Which is the law that attracts and gives
Where everything obeys and everything lives.

C. Emmanuel Griffin

More Than We Need

If the brain contains grains of wheat
Like words we meet through the concourse of our lives,
Then we have stored within our minds enough to feed
The nation's poor and give them a bag of their own for planting
We must remember that the creator connects
All who tap into the network intended to allow
Work to be done in time, and power to be produced to move
All that is alive to pursue more of what is needed to survive and thrive
We indeed are the seed that brings about fruit with care
We are enough planted in the soil where we were dropped
Regardless of the germination process endured
All we must do is connect with invisible appendages
That allow for the flow of thought and into this world
A new meaning will be brought
Its currency like water or air will flow though all
With capacity to spare and then and there we will know
That we were made to reap and sow
For the building of a foundation that will support a nation
Without the limitation of imaginary borders
Where outlawed will be the currency hoarders who steal
That which was intended to be shared
There is more than enough if we use the stuff
That we have been given and waste not a single atom
Of that which we through knowledge understand is
The author of want and the purveyor of need
With this each of our minds are freed to expand
Into the space without the gravity of land
Because our coming together is not by force or fear,
We enter into a common place to uniformly
See the world through the eyes of all sojourners of humanity.

More Than We Need

C. Emmanuel Griffin

The Math

There are only two functions in life, plus zero
There is only addition and subtraction
They are given different names
Plus or minus, giving or taking, lending or borrowing
Coming or going, here or there, in or out, on or off
The list is endless
Look at the world differently
Through this lens of simplicity for a while and
You will see a different reality: to have is to give, to die is to live
If you want the things of Heaven, then give up the things of Hell
If you want the rewards of freedom, then give up the activities of jail
If you want a place to be silent, then listen
At your fingertips, within your memory's grip you hold
The key to your salvation
No matter your station
Relativity is real, and it is just a perspective God is real
And God gives you no directive except this:
Do what you must, love the Lord with your mind, body and soul
Love your neighbor as yourself
This is it all
This is the blueprint
This is where East meets West and North meets South
This is where you can see the whole universe from inside and out
This is where you can witness the birth of time
In all things there is growth and decay and one day
Our sun will pass away but be the time far or near
Never, ever, give into fear, because there is no end of the story
Because there is no beginning of the story
There is only the mission
When you find it, pursue it
Never let it out of your mind's sight for a second
Inhale and exhale, this is the movement
Build up or tear down, this is improvement
Just know that all that is, you deserve
There is none more deserving than you
You, through your ancestors, have given for centuries
Into and to those that have given so much
and infinite return is due.

The Math

C. Emmanuel Griffin

See

God said come sit with me
Dip your toes in the eternal stream
View the force of time as I do
Everything is subject to
The flow of it by different names
It is the value vault
Use it wisely and accumulate
Lose it foolishly and life will halt
Some seek more
Some seek to travel back and forth
Nothing is impossible if you believe
All things have a cost to call
Energy is a game of redirection
Change is but a recycling
Death as you named it is as well
Look closely and you will experience
Heaven inside yourself

In His Words

A galaxy is amazing to man
For one with vision it's a grain of sand
The Word is the greatest gift of man
It is the currency of exchange
Through which earthy and heavenly events change
And continents are rearranged
Organized by different names
Lines drawn by imagination
Dividing what one cannot rightfully own
Only the unjust in body and soul
Seek to forcefully control
The internal workings of another temple
They corrupt the worship
And are ignorant
To the fact that the earth is the mothership
And it is powered by the word expressed

C. Emmanuel Griffin

The fearful kill what they cannot control
And mis-assign authorship
Shaking themselves to sleep
Imbibing substances that
weaken the moral foundation
Leading to the unjust confiscation
of knowledge of word and action
Will they learn will they turn
If not, they will burn
And again I will begin again
The grave for the body
Heaven for the spirit
Are your respective homes
Find the river
Find the stream
Image the nation
Of your dreams
Watch in amazement
At what will be
Stay with me
And See.

See

Nothing

Nothing is but something not yet realized
Everything that is anything was made by you and I
We are the dust of stars coalesced into our current form
We are one with the Creator who lives as spirits do
Our making and undertaking
Are the breaking of new ground
Our movement and music are the light and speed of sound
All that is at some point was not and can
Become again Everyone is someone, as everywhere is somewhere
But only relative to that of another aligned
And in our taking this space we are staking
Let us remember the code
Possible is impossible in a world without you
So please, do whatever you choose and be
Go wherever you desire to be found
And embrace the life and retrace the line
That best resembles your truth told in telling times
There is but one correct answer to life's question when put to the test
It is the permission you seek to chase your wildest ideals and dreams
It is the word most perfectly blessed
Make something out of nothing you must because
The answer, the only answer, is YES.

Nothing

C. Emmanuel Griffin

The Soul

The spirit of loss is an albatross
The spirit of gain burdens the brain
Wisdom is knowledge of the Holy One
Let us be wise in all our getting
Let us invite a spirit of cooperation
and collaboration into all our pursuits and cohabitations
The body houses the soul and the spirit fills its shell
Get wisdom and discernment they will serve you well
You belong to God and Jesus
Christ is in you
He left the Holy Spirit to comfort you
There is a place and unlimited space
With room for selectivity and creativity of life and its direction
There is no course or preset destination
There is no direction defined or inclined
There is only the desire of your chosen view
What you will see combinative-ly will be
The unraveling of a dimension of reality
Some may struggle to achieve
The depth of thought to conceive
As space and time unwind
Unfolding as a children's nursery rhyme
Each step each meter pressed on as light
At speeds beyond our Earthly sight
Where coded dreams can only keep pace
And finally, we observe God's infinite face
Branded and blinded to the untruth that binds
Filled with the spirits that good memories find
Free as freedom given in a ring
A vision a glimpse of eternity's everything
All bundled into the space of the unseen
Held in place by the Force of Faith
Where all understand that Time is Space.

The Soul

Author Biography

C. Emmanuel Griffin is a teacher, from a long line of teachers/educators and preachers, who enjoys the challenge of working with children and adults and helping them construct the tools to draw out their deepest truth and understand that they are literally the drivers of their destiny.

He believes that each of us is directly connected to the creative spirit and all we must do is tap in, sit still and allow the unlimited resources of the universe pass through. And if we are wise, we will capture what we can with our gifted receptors, minds and hands, to share with those who choose to join us along life's journey.

Artist Biography

Graham Goddard is a visual artist exploring creativity through various artistic mediums including painting, site-specific installations and mixed media. Goddard has exhibited at the Skirball Museum, the California African American Museum, and in numerous art galleries throughout the United States and internationally.

www.ingramcontent.com/pod-product-compliance
Lightning Source LLC
Chambersburg PA
CBHW021349090426
42742CB00008B/796